A Tale Of Two Teddies

BIG BEAR HUGS!

2019

Acknowledgements

Dick Frantz, Steiff Historian
for giving me photos and anecdotes of Margarete Steiff

Dr. John Gable, Director, Theodore Roosevelt Association
for sharing his "teddy bear files" with me

Judith Izen, author of "Collector's Guide to Ideal Dolls"
for her in-depth knowledge of the Michtoms and Ideal

Krystyna Poray Goddu, my editor
for imparting her expertise and enthusiasm to this project

Susan Schulman and Christine Morin, my agents
for their patience with a first-time author

The Writer's Group
for mentoring an artist who aspired to be a writer

My Family and Friends
for their tireless support and encouragement

And to my husband, Jack
for giving me the opportunity to devote myself
to my art and writing for the past five years

First edition/Eighth printing
Copyright © 2001, 2002, 2003, 2004, 2005, 2006, 2008, 2010 Kathleen Bart

This book was originally published by Portfolio Press Corporation.

To purchase additional copies of this book,
please contact: Reverie Publishing Company
130 South Wineow St., Cumberland, MD 21502
888-721-4999 www.reveriepublishing.com

Library of Congress Control Number
2004099915

ISBN 978-1-932485-23-3

Printed and bound in Korea

A Tale Of Two Teddies

The First Teddy Bears Tell Their True Stories

Kathleen Bart

Reverie
PUBLISHING COMPANY

in memory of
my mother, Joan, who first instilled my love of books,
and my mother-in-law, Judy,
who encouraged the creation of this book

J ust over a century ago, cuddly teddy bears had not yet been invented. Back then, toy bears were either carved of hard wood, cast in cold metal or stitched in itchy wool. Their paws had claws and their mouths had teeth, just like those of wild bears.

Thank goodness, someone was inspired to invent the soft stuffed teddy bear we know today! In fact, *two* different people in *two* distant parts of the world ... America and Germany ... created this furry friend at the same time. Made of mohair plush, this new toy had jointed limbs, bright button eyes and a smiling stitched mouth.

Experts argue over which teddy bear was the very first. So do the bears! Now that more than one hundred years have passed, *each bear* wants to present his side of the story, as he recalls it. Then it will be up to you to decide:

Which one was the first teddy bear?

A Bear Is Born: God Bless America!

I was the first soft stuffed teddy bear, born in 1902 in the good old U.S.A. My home town was Brooklyn, New York. I lived in the front window of a candy store on Tompkins Avenue, right in the thick of things. Outside my window, the street bustled with people rushing in all directions, pausing only to shop from pushcart peddlers. Hands flew as they gestured, bargaining back and forth in the languages of their homelands. You see, people came from all over the world to live here. It was a place where anyone could achieve anything.

Birth of a Bear: Dear Deutschland

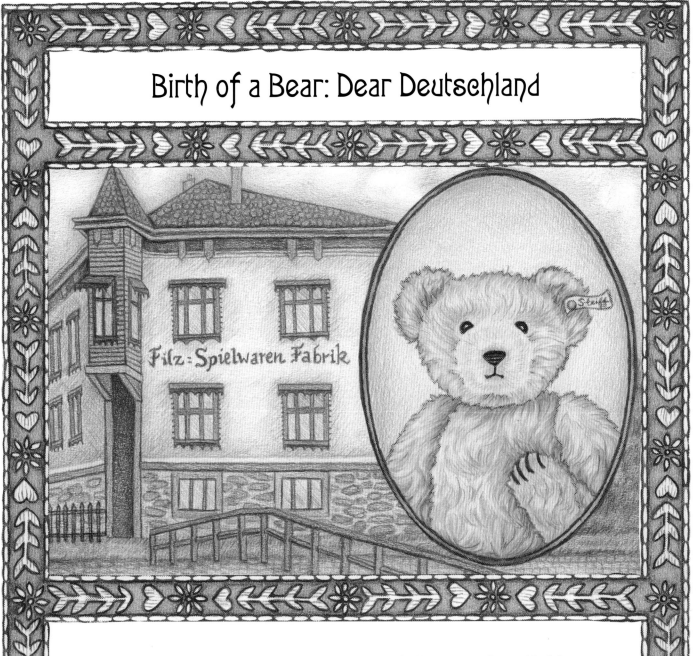

I beg to differ, *mein* friend. I was *der* first fully jointed stuffed bear, born in Germany in 1902. I resided in a toy maker's workshop in a charming village called Giengen, whose artisans were world famous for the detail and quality of their work. Giengen's skilled craftspeople could be heard carving, hammering, and sanding from morning until night. The town square boasted the shops of the finest clockmakers, woodcarvers and toy makers. Naturally, the first teddy bear would come from the toy-making center of the world, *ja*?

Father of the First Teddy Bear

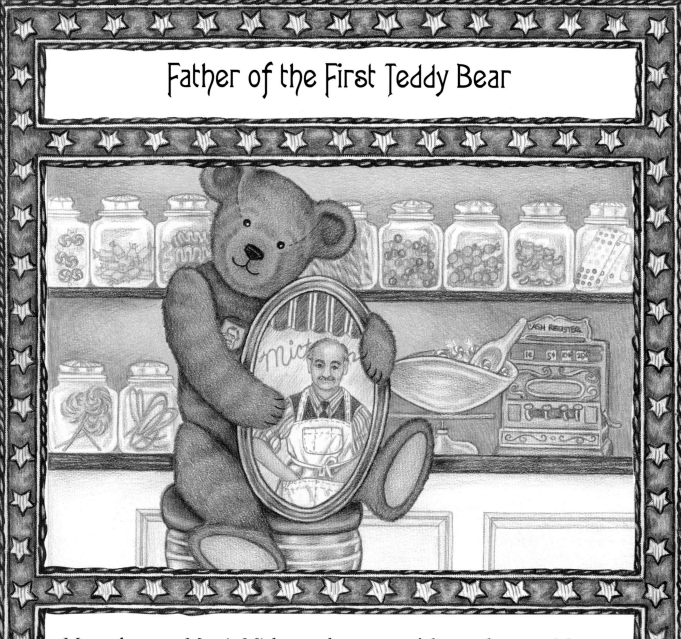

My maker was Morris Michtom, the owner of the candy store. Mo, as I liked to call him, was a Lithuanian immigrant. He had arrived in Brooklyn in 1889 with a dream of having a shop all his own. Starting a business while learning a new language was tough. Competition was stiff, with stores on every corner. But Mo was a real go-getter, always on the lookout for the latest novelty to sell in his store. If nothing struck his fancy, he would dream up something new. Then, with the help of his wife Rose, he would make it himself. Soon, Mo and Rose built a business they could be proud of.

Mother Of The First Teddy Bear

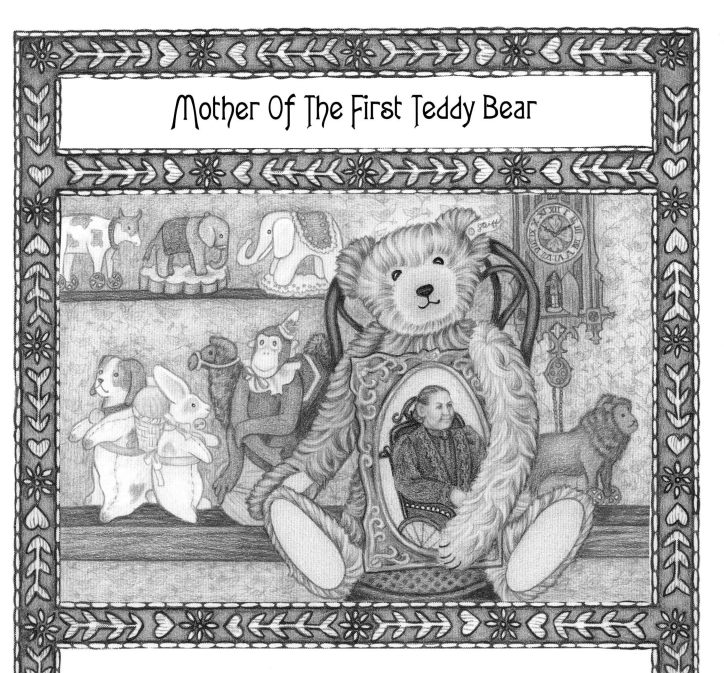

Mein creator was a toy maker named Margarete Steiff. *Fraulein* Steiff's first toys were small felt elephants. They became so popular that she formed her own toy company in 1880. This was a remarkable accomplishment, as women were rarely business owners at that time. Fraulein Steiff's confinement to a wheelchair made her task even more challenging. In spite of these obstacles, she developed such a successful business that she had to hire additional artisans, including her creative nephew, *Herr* Richard Steiff.

Inspiration! Bully!

One November morning in 1902, a cartoon in the newspaper caught Mo's eye. It showed President Teddy Roosevelt refusing to shoot a trapped bear during one of his hunting trips. Bada Bing Bada Boom! The cartoon gave Mo a great idea! He would make a *soft stuffed toy bear* and name it "Teddy's Bear." His store would be the first to have such a novelty. Mo and Rose sewed my body and movable paws out of plush fabric. To make it official, Mo wrote to President Roosevelt, asking if he could name the very first stuffed bear after him. I sure would feel important if I were named after the President of the whole United States!

Inspiration! Wunderbär!

Meanwhile, far away in Germany, Richard got a splendid idea while sketching bears at the Stuttgart Zoo. Children needed a furry friend to cuddle, like a *soft stuffed toy bear*, perhaps. He and Fraulein Steiff designed me of genuine mohair and stuffed me with the finest excelsior. Shoe buttons were selected for my eyes, shiny and black. It took several tries to get my jointed limbs to move just right. Finally satisfied, they named me *"Bär"* or "Bear" in English. They proudly proclaimed me the world's first stuffed bear. However, I wasn't known as a "Teddy Bär" until several years later when I became popular in America.

Voted Most Popular

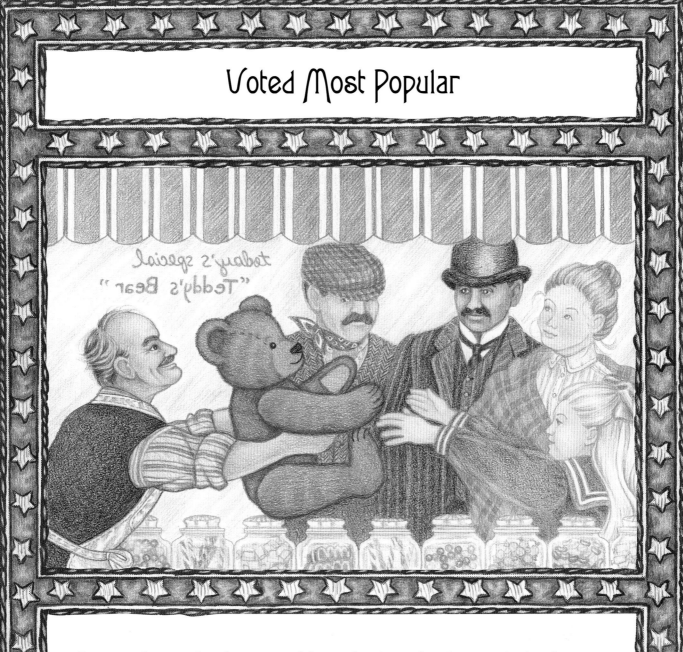

I'll never forget the day Mo told me the President's permission letter arrived. Mo was so thrilled that he dropped what he was doing and ran to place me in the store window. Right next to me, he placed a sign introducing me as "Teddy's Bear." People bustling past the store stopped in their tracks to admire me. Boy, did I love the limelight! Everyone wanted a Teddy Bear just like me. Mo and Rose had to sew more and more bears. I've always wondered if I would have been as popular if I wasn't named after President Theodore Roosevelt.

Late Bloomer

A Bär by any other name is still a Bär. Quality matters much more than a name. But quality comes with a price and I'm afraid I fetched quite a few *deutschmarks*. At first, people were hesitant to spend a large sum of money on a toy bear. But Fraulein Steiff insisted that "only the best is good enough for children." Many parents appreciated the quality and craftsmanship of the Steiff bears. They wanted their children to have the best and were willing to pay more for it. A loyal group of admirers quickly began to form.

All the President's Bears

Talk about being in the right place at the right time! In 1904, I became the unofficial mascot for President Roosevelt's re-election campaign. Once he began his second term, I became a national hero. Teddy Bear mania swept America! Every American, young and old, wanted one. Mo and Rose sold their store and devoted themselves to manufacturing Teddy Bears full time. They named their business the "Ideal Toy and Novelty Company." Mo sure came a long way from being a small shop owner. He was soon the head of one of the biggest toy companies in the whole wide world!

Presentation Is Everything

In 1903, I made my grand debut at the famous Leipzig Toy Fair. On the very last day, I charmed an American buyer into ordering 3,000 Steiff bears, ending the fair with a bang! Quite a coup! Inspired by this splendid response, Richard worked night and day to perfect my design. He created imaginative displays starring moi...yours truly! Then Fraulein Steiff sent us to open a brand-new showroom in New York. If you can make it there, you can make it anywhere. Look out New York, I have arrived!

A Teddy In Every Home

FAST BLACK SKIRT CO.
109 East 124th Street, NEW YORK CITY
MANUFACTURERS OF
Electric Bright Eye Teddy Bears

It wasn't long before other companies started to cash in on the Teddy Bear craze. They knocked off Mo's idea and made copies of jointed stuffed bears that looked just like me. Some were made right in America, while others were imported from Europe. Even worse, all these stuffed bears became known as "Teddy Bears!" But I know I was the only bear who had official permission to use this name. Those copycats really made my fur curl!

Bärenjahre: The Bear Years

WED·AT NOON TO-DAY.

WHITE HOUSE DECORATED

All Ready for the Marriage of Miss
Roosevelt and Mr. Longworth.

The moment we opened our New York showroom, we were flooded with "Teddy Bär" orders. Once I got used to the name, I rather enjoyed my new celebrity status as "Teddy Bär." According to Steiff family legend, Steiff Teddy Bärs were ordered as centerpieces for the wedding of President Roosevelt's "Princess" daughter. But the real feather in our cap was selling almost a million bears between 1903 and 1907! Now that's legendary! We called this period *"Bärenjahre"* or "The Bear Years."

Mo and The Missing Letter

Why send to Europe
for your
Jointed Animals
*When you can buy them right here at
half the price?*

Our Bear is an exact reproduction of the foreign model.

The Ideal Line of Bears, Cats and Rabbi...

IDEAL NOVELTY COMPA...

Lowest prices on the market for goods of this quality

Other Teddy Bear companies, jealous of Mo's big business, started a nasty rumor. They claimed the permission letter was a big fat lie. Mo searched and searched for the letter to prove it was real, but he couldn't find it. I felt like the rug was snatched right out from under me. Now I had no way to prove I was the first Official Teddy Bear. Anyway, in spite of not having the letter, I am still regarded as the first Teddy Bear by many people, especially Americans. So there! How do you like them apples?!

"Knopf Im Ohr" Button In Ear

I was insulted when other Teddy Bear companies had the nerve to accuse Fraulein Steiff of copying Mo's teddy bear. Rubbish! The truth is, other Teddy Bear manufacturers began to copy *me*! In fact, Fraulein Steiff had to create a trademark "button in ear" to identify her Teddy Bears as authentic Steiffs. The "button in ear" became the symbol of quality sought by collectors around the globe. Harrumph!

Put Your Own Two Cents In!

Enough already! Now that you've got the inside scoop, you've probably made up your mind about who was first...Teddy Bär, or me, Teddy Bear. Or maybe you've decided that we were *both* the first. It is possible that Fraulien Steiff and Mo had the same idea at the same time. No matter what anyone thinks, I'll always believe I was the first Teddy Bear. But it's a free country. Everyone's entitled to their own opinion. Sometimes, you have to just agree to disagree.

The Granddaddies of all Teddies

Although it's obvious that I was first, this bickering is becoming boring! Regardless of which one of us came first, we *both* share the honor of being the Forefathers of all Teddy Bears. As the first of our kind, we are the proud Granddaddies of millions of Teddy Bear descendants throughout the globe. Arguing is not proper conduct for bears of our noble position. What would Fraulein Steiff and Morris Michtom think of us? Out of respect for our creators, let's declare a truce, once and for all! *Wunderbär!*

My Ideal Family Tree

Shirley Temple Doll
1934

It took 28 tries to capture Shirley's likeness. The toy makers walked through the streets of Brooklyn with different doll heads until little girls exclaimed: "That's Shirley Temple!"

Doll-Faced Teddy Bear 1950

This cute little fella had a doll-like look because of his molded vinyl face and round plastic "spangle" eyes.

Unjointed Teddy Bear
1942

Like many modern teddies, this one has arms and legs that are sewn into one postion.

Cartoon-Eyed Bear
1914

Mo designed this bear's expressive eyes after Clifford Berryman's cartoon bears.

Smokey The Bear

1953

A Bear With A Cause! Ideal managed to get the exclusive rights to create Smokey The Bear and spread the word about preventing forest fires: "Remember... only YOU can prevent forest fires!"

Campbell Soup Kids

1955

Ideal created toys to tie in with food products like Campbell's Soup. Mmm! Mmm! Good!

75th Anniversary

1978

Ideal created a fancy replica of me, the original bear, to celebrate my 75th birthday. Sadly, this was one of the very last Ideal teddy bears ever made.

So What Became Of The Ideal Toy Company?

Quite a character!
Morris Michtom knew he was onto something big when he created me and named me after Teddy Roosevelt. He had discovered a secret to success… celebrities sell toys! As early as 1907, Mo began to create toys based on popular cartoon characters and products like Cracker Jack and Campbell's Soup.

Oh, You Beautiful Doll!
By 1909 Mo was the biggest teddy bear maker in America, but he refused to sit on his duff! The Ideal Novelty and Toy Company branched out into dollmaking. As for me, I remain partial to teddy bears.

The Unbreakables
Mo believed that toys were meant for playing, not for sitting on shelves. After witnessing his daughter's tears when she accidentally broke her ceramic doll, Mo was determined to make Ideal toys unbreakable. He began to try new materials which where not only more durable, but more affordable.

Art Imitates Life
Mo designed Ideal toys to be as lifelike as possible. Always the innovator, Mo created amusing gimmicks like voices that squealed "mama" and eyes that fluttered. He even created a doll named "Betsy Wetsy," which wet her diapers after drinking from her baby bottle. That's not exactly my cup of tea. I guess I have a "dry" sense of humor. But, hey, whatever floats your boat!

Like Father, Like Son

In 1923, Mo's son, Benjamin, followed in his dad's footsteps. He joined Ideal and helped the family business thrive. Together Mo and Ben ushered Ideal into its Golden Era, which spanned more than 30 years. Ben took charge of the company when Mo passed away in 1938.

Hooray For Hollywood!

Ben was a real go-getter just like his dad. He was not the least bit shy about schmoozing with the stars of the silver screen to secure celebrity endorsements for Ideal toys. Ben even had the chutzpah to hob nob in Hollywood until he clinched a deal for the creation of a Shirley Temple doll.

Hello Everyone in TV Land!

Ideal sponsored the very first televised Macy's Thanksgiving Day Parade. Ideal was also one of the first toy companies to advertise its products during children's Saturday morning T.V. programs.

End of an Era

Ben passed away in 1980, just two years after celebrating Ideal's 75th anniversary. In 1982, Ben's son Mark sold the Ideal Novelty and Toy Company. Ideal teddy bears were never to be made again.

The Legend Lives On

Still, Ideal toys live on in the memories of adults who remain nostalgic for the playthings of their youth. Old Ideal toys are eagerly sought-after at toy shows and auctions. The story of Mo's success continues to inspire enterprising individuals with ambition and a dream.

My Steiff Descendants

Bär Dolly

1913

This playful lad was produced in red, white and blue for the U.S. election in 1913.

Alphonso

1908

The Grand Duke of Russia commissioned the Steiffs to make this exotic bear as a gift for his daughter, Princess Xenia Georgievna.

Jocko

1922

Monkeys were one of Steiff's earliest and most popular stuffed animals, second only to teddy bärs, of course.

Elephant

1930

Designed for Steiff's 50th jubilee, this felt elephant was a replica of the very first stuffed animal *Fraulein Steiff* made in 1880.

Guardsman

1936

The famous toy store, FAO Schwarz, often commissions exclusive toys from Steiff. This Guardsman was one of the very first.

Steiff — The oldest plush-toy company in the world!

Millennium Bär

2000

This fellow celebrates the continuing Steiff tradition into the new Millennium!

Original Teddy

1966

This bear sure changed with the times! His shaved muzzle gives him a modern look.

Jackie Baby

1953

He reminds me of when I was just a cub! This baby bear was designed for my 50th birthday.

The Margarete Steiff Toy Company Today

Persistence Beats Resistance
I'm not surprised that The Margarete Steiff Toy Company is still in business today. Mein creator, Margarete Steiff, perservered in the face of challenge throughout her life.

A Stitch In Time
Sewing was a challenge because of a partially paralyzed hand, yet Fraulein Steiff perservered. She soon mastered the art and bought the first sewing machine in all of Giengen. Sewing became the means to her livelihood and the key to her independence.

A True Perfectionist
Fraulein Steiff insisted on making each original sample before handing it off to a worker to duplicate. She held her employees to the same high standards she set for herself.

Only The Best Is Good Enough For Children
Inspired by her affection for the neighborhood *kinder*, Fraulein Steiff began to sew soft toys. Her desire to touch the lives of children formed the foundation of a lasting business.

A Family Affair
Fraulein Steiff developed and utilized her nephews' talents. She worked most closely with Richard, whose creative spirit inspired the development of me, the teddy bär! Paul's drafting skills were perfect for pattern making. Franz, Otto and Hugo handled the business end of toy making.

Tough Times

Fraulein Steiff passed away in 1909. Her nephews vowed to continue the company according to the principles of their beloved aunt. The war times that followed were a challenge for the Steiffs. Richard, Paul and Hugo were called to serve in the armed forces in World War I. During World War II, the toy factory was forced to make war supplies. Toy production resumed after the war, thanks to company archives, which had been cleverly packed and hidden.

Let The Good Times Roll!

In the 1960s and 1970s, the Steiffs maintained their artistic integrity despite the popularity of cheap bears that began to flood the mass market. They were rewarded by the loyalty of collectors who valued toys of high quality. The Margarete Steiff Toy Company proudly celebrated its one-hundredth anniversary in 1980.

Steiff Stands The Test of Time

Steiff animals are still crafted by hand as they were more than one hundred years ago. The Steiff "button in ear" still stands for fine materials and realistic detail. The Margarete Steiff Toy Company remains the oldest plush toy company in the world. Fraulein Steiff left a legacy that continues to touch the lives of children today.

Hundredth Birthday Bash

Despite our affectionate squabbling, we shared many adventures during our first one hundred years. But we never dreamed that one day we would celebrate our hundredth birthday bash together! It was a celebration shared by teddy bear lovers around the globe, and a wonderful start to a new century together.

Teddy bear lovers will forever
cherish the world's most enduring
toy. As everyone knows, teddy
bears are more than just toys. They
become lifelong companions from
the very moment they are placed
in a child's crib until the day they
are passed down to the next
generation. Warm memories,
friendship and love will forever
be the legacy of the teddy bear.

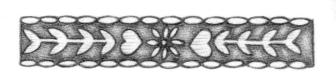

JUST MARRIED